# RACHMANINOFF

## FANTASY PIECES
(Morceaux de Fantaisie)

OPUS 3
FOR THE PIANO

Murray Baylor, Editor



## CONTENTS



Second Edition


*Cover art:* Golden Autumn, *1895*
*by Isaac Levitan (1860–1900)*
*Tretyakov Gallery, Moscow, Russia*
*Scala/Art Resource, New York*

# FOREWORD

## *SERGEI VASILYEVICH RACHMANINOFF*

(April 2, 1873—March 21, 1943)

## *THE MAN*

Rachmaninoff was born in the Novgorod district of Russia in 1873, the year that Debussy became 10 years old and Liszt 61. Both his father and mother belonged to the upper class of Russian society and had inherited large holdings of land. The father, a military officer, was a charming person—warm and loving toward his children but addicted to gambling and riotous living. The mother, a rather stern person, seemed to do her duty somewhat coldly by her six children. The father's behavior eventually caused the ruin of the family fortune, and Rachmaninoff's parents had to sell their last estate and move to St. Petersburg (now Leningrad) the year that Sergei was nine years old—in 1882. A short time later the parents separated, the children staying with their mother.

The boy's extraordinary musical gifts had already been discovered and encouraged by good training, so that he received a scholarship at the St. Petersburg Conservatory shortly after the family moved to that city. Unfortunately his motivation at that time didn't match his talent, and he failed to take his work very seriously. His mother, concerned about his further education, consulted his older cousin, Alexander Siloti, who had just returned from a period of study with Liszt and was beginning his career as a piano virtuoso. Siloti said that he would recommend the boy to Nicolai Zverev, who had been his own teacher, and urged the mother to send her son to Moscow to work under the strict discipline of Zverev, who taught gifted young pianists in the lower levels of instruction at the Moscow Conservatory. A few students lived in Zverev's home, had their lessons there, and had their practice supervised by the professor and his sister. Rachmaninoff went to the Zverev house in the fall of 1885, when he was 12, and lived and studied there for four years. While under Zverev's tutelage he not only developed his pianistic ability through expert training and well-directed practice, but he also heard the extraordinary series of historical recitals of keyboard music given by Anton Rubenstein and became acquainted with many important Russian musicians, among them Tchaikowsky. When Rachmaninoff left the Zverev house and entered the upper level courses at the Moscow Conservatory he studied piano with Siloti, counterpoint with Taniev, and composition with Arensky in a class that included Alexander Scriabin. Rachmaninoff graduated from the conservatory a year earlier than most students—at the age of 19—and was given a rarely awarded "great gold medal" of the conservatory, having finished with highest honors in both piano and composition.

From his early maturity to the middle of his life Rachmaninoff had a variety of experiences as a free artist, making the best of opportunities, and struggling with personal problems. His music was published almost as soon as he graduated from the conservatory, partly on the strength of Tchaikowsky's enthusiasm for it, and he continued to compose while earning a rather insecure living as accompanist, piano soloist, and conductor. His one-act opera *Aleko*, written as a final examination in composition at the conservatory, was produced by the Bolshoi Opera in 1893 and was praised by Tchaikowsky who heard the first performance. The friendship and encouragement of the older man meant a great deal to the 20-year-old Rachmaninoff, but the premiere of his opera was little more than six months past when Tchaikowsky died at the age of 53.

In 1895 Rachmaninoff started to compose his first symphony, a work he hoped would enhance his growing reputation, but when the symphony was played for the first time in 1897 in St. Petersburg the critics were merciless. They didn't realize that, in part, their impression of the work was a result of inadequate rehearsal and a poor performance. Rachmaninoff was so discouraged by this fiasco that he was depressed for months. He refused to have the work repeated under more favorable circumstances; indeed it was never played again during his lifetime. Though his fame was growing, and he was invited to London to play and conduct his music, he continued to brood over the disastrous premiere of his first large work for orchestra alone. He had begun to work on his second piano concerto, scheduled for a first performance in London the following season, but had reached an impasse and found himself unable to continue an excellent beginning. A friend suggested he consult Dr. Nicolai Dahl, a physician and amateur musician who had treated emotional illness successfully with suggestion and hypnosis. He began to see Dr. Dahl daily in January of 1900. A few months later his artistic impotence was cured, and he was able to finish the ever-popular C minor concerto which he dedicated to Dr. Dahl.

The year 1902 marked a major change in his life because in that year, when he was 29, he married his cousin, Natalya Satina. A year later their first daughter was born. He conducted at the Bolshoi Opera from 1904 to 1906 while working on two operas of his own, but unsatisfactory production conditions at the opera house and the political unrest following the 1905 revolution led him to move with his family to Dresden where he was better able to work on new compositions. In 1909 he came to the United States to play and conduct his music, particularly the new third piano concerto which he played with the New York Philharmonic Orchestra under Walter Damrosch. While in the United States he was offered the conductorship of the Boston Symphony Orchestra which had become vacant, but he refused. After his experience in the United States he returned to Russia to continue conducting, visited England again to play and conduct, and had a brief stay in Rome in 1913. In spite of the advantages of living in Germany or Italy the Rachmaninoffs preferred to make their home in Russia.

The Russian revolution of 1917 led to the greatest change of all in the life of the Rachmaninoff family. They were in Russia at the time of the Czar's abdication and the resulting political upheavals. While the turmoil was at its height, Rachmaninoff received an invitation to play recitals in Sweden, with the likelihood of repeating them in other Scandinavian countries. Unsure of what the future might hold in Russia, he obtained a permit to leave the country for these performances and to take his family with him. One cold night just before Christmas in 1917 the Rachmaninoffs crossed the border of Russia to go through Finland to Stockholm. They were never to return to their homeland. Their only possesions were on their backs or in their luggage; everything else they owned, including their beautiful estate at Ivanovka, had been confiscated by the communist authorities.

Rachmaninoff was in debt and had a wife and two little daughters to provide for. He decided that playing the piano was the best way he could provide a livelihood for his family and set about becoming a piano virtuoso. He was 45 years old, his technique was rusty, and his repertory limited, since up to that time his public performances had most often been of his own music. But he immediately began to prepare for a different kind of life and let it be known that he wanted engagements as a piano recitalist. This was the beginning of almost 25 years of the suitcase existence of a solo musician. Enticing offers soon came from the United States, so he crossed the Atlantic a second time, arriving in New York with his family just as the first World War came to an end.

Since they were afraid to return to Russia the family led a rather nomadic existence. Sometimes their home was New York, sometimes Dresden, sometimes a suburb of Paris. As an international concert artist Rachmaninoff usually accepted engagements in the fall and early winter in Europe and on the American continent in the late winter and early spring. Travel by train and ocean liner was time-consuming and exhausting, and there was always the necessity of practicing. He accepted a few invitations to conduct his own orchestral works but again refused to become the conductor of the Boston Symphony Orchestra, and rejected a similar offer from Cincinnati. There was now no time nor energy for composition except during summers, when the concert season was over, and his practice time could be reduced to a minimum. In 1931 the Rachmaninoffs bought property near Lake Lucerne in Switzerland and built a home there. The summers seemed idyllic in these beautiful surroundings, especially when they could have expatriate countrymen join them for all-Russian weekends or week-long parties.

The family finally sold their home in Switzerland and, after a summer in California, bought a new home in Beverly Hills. Because of recurring health problems Rachmaninoff had decided that the season of 1942-1943 would end his concertizing. He was able to carry out only part of a planned tour; his recital in Knoxville, Tennessee, in February of 1943 was the last time he played. The remainder of the tour had to be cancelled, and he returned to California where he died of cancer a few days before his 70th birthday. He had become a citizen of the United States shortly before his death.

Just as there are different evaluations of Rachmaninoff the pianist and Rachmaninoff the composer, there were apparent contradictions between the man and the artist. Rachmaninoff had the reputation of being a cold person—one whose thoughts and feelings were hidden behind a mask. He avoided publicity and interviewers if at all possible. He was slow to speak and notably stingy with words. When he walked on a stage to play a concert—a tall, gaunt, solemn man with rather Mongolian features and the haircut of a convict—his demeanor was indeed austere (Stravinsky once characterized him as a "six-and-a-half-foot-scowl"). For a great deal of his life he was in ill health and suffering from neuralgia. He never felt comfortable expressing himself in English, and with strangers, or when he was in public, he usually felt ill at ease. Friends who saw him at a party when he was feeling well and speaking Russian, found him warm, witty, and bubbling with laughter and high spirits. Similarly, in a recital, after he began to play, one had a very different impression listening to the music he produced. Absolute technical perfection was the rule, but in addition, his tone was sensuously beautiful, his phrasing elegant and free, and his rhythms incisive but flexible. In his playing as in his compositions the man behind the mask was revealed as a sensitive, outgoing person.

## *THE MUSIC*

A story is told about a woman at a cocktail party who asked a rising young pianist about his forthcoming New York recital. When he told her that his program would include a group of Rachmaninoff preludes she replied, "Did you say Rachmaninoff preludes? Oh, did he write more than one?" The story may not be true, but it points up the fact that when many people hear Rachmaninoff's name they think of the famous C-sharp minor prelude, and sometimes they know little more about his music. This piece, written when the composer was just out of the conservatory, brought him early international fame, and it has become one of the most popular piano pieces written in the last hundred years. Its immediate success can be explained in part by the fact that it was sold outright, for a fee worth about $20, to a publisher who didn't get an international copyright. In a short time and ever since, it has appeared in all kinds of editions—some of them titled *The Bells of Moscow*, *The Burning of Moscow*, *The Moscow Waltz*, and even *That Moscow Rag*. For a time the piece was played too frequently—often quite badly—and its composer grew to dislike playing it because it was demanded as an encore at all his piano recitals before the audience would leave the hall. But there are reasons for its popularity other than its ready availability. It is clearly an original, striking, effectively developed musical idea which makes a dramatic impact on the listeners when it is beautifully played.

Rachmaninoff wrote a great deal of other music and probably would have written still more if he had not had careers as conductor and pianist as well as composer. His works include operas, symphonies, symphonic poems, vocal-symphonic music, chamber music, works for piano and orchestra, unaccompanied choral music, music for piano ensemble, over 80 songs, transcriptions of music by other composers, and, needless to say, a great deal of original piano music.

The solo piano music was largely written before 1917 so that most of it has been played and heard for over 65 years without showing signs of reaching retirement age. The most important works in this category began with the five pieces in this edition published as opus 3 and fashionably entitled *Morceaux de Fantaisie* (Fantasy Pieces). Both the *Mélodie* (No. 3), and *Sérénade* (No. 5) were revised (made much more elaborate and difficult) by Rachmaninoff in 1940. However, this edition includes these two selections in their original versions.

The next solo piano works to follow were the seven pieces in opus 10, entitled *Morceaux de Salon*, and six pieces of opus 16 called *Moments Musicaux*. There are two sonatas, two large sets of variations, two sets of *Etudes-Tableaux* opus 33 and opus 39, and 24 preludes in all the major and minor keys. Unlike the 24 preludes of Chopin, Rachmaninoff's, on the whole, are longer; were published at three different times; and are not arranged in one orderly key sequence. The most famous one, the C-sharp minor prelude, is part of opus 3, published in 1892. The next 10 appeared in 1903 as opus 23, and the remaining 13 were published in 1910 as opus 32. There are a few other pieces of less interest and minor significance, some of which were written as student exercises.

The only work for solo piano which dates from the later part of Rachmaninoff's life is the *Variations on a Theme of Corelli* op. 42. This work, published in 1931, was played that year for the first time by Rachmaninoff in Montreal. Actually the theme used for variations in this set was not by Corelli but is a melody known as *La Folia* which was common property of a number of 18th century composers. The work is an ingenious set of variations with many of the same characteristics as the dazzling variations on a Paganini theme for piano and orchestra written in 1934, and finally entitled *Rhapsody on a Theme of Paganini*, op. 43.

## THIS EDITION

This edition of *Fantasy Pieces*, opus 3 is based on the first editions corrected by the composer and the versions found in *The Complete Works of Rachmaninoff* published in the Soviet Union since 1949. Most of the existing autographs of Rachmaninoff's works are in libraries in Russia, and Soviet librarians are uncooperative about letting foreigners have access to them. The editors of the Russian complete edition who had the use of the manuscripts, however, were very competent and have produced a valuable Urtext, though there are misprints, and the number of copies is severely limited. Obvious errors have been corrected without comment in this edition. Controversial passages are so noted on the pages where they appear.

Rachmaninoff seldom wrote metronome marks for his piano music except for the preludes of opus 23. Both before and after that publication of 1903 he apparently thought it better not to be as specific as possible about tempos. Most musicians agree that the precise tempo for a performance should be governed to a degree by the instrument, the resonance of the room, and the taste and skill of the player. Rachmaninoff probably would have accepted modifications of his metronome marks.

For these pieces that have no metronome marks from the composer the suggested metronome marks are indicated thus: ( ♩ = c. 80). The fingering given here is largely new. Rachmaninoff wrote fairly complete fingerings for a few of his pieces (though not for any in this collection), but for the most part he wrote fingering only for unusual or particularly complex passages. Some of his fingering is excellent for anyone, but since he was a tall man with king-size hands some of his fingerings are impractical for small or average hands. There will never be agreement about the best fingering for many passages because such judgments are based on the size and flexibility of the hands, on previous training, and on the old habits of different individuals. The fingerings offered here are serviceable for the average size hand, and some facilitations incorporated in this edition will ease some of the playing difficulties. No apology is offered for these; if one can play all the notes the composer wrote in an easier rather than a harder way and achieve equally good musical results, the learning process will be shorter and the performance more secure. Concert artists take advantage of such helps; why should students not do so as well? Fingerings from any source should be regarded as suggestions for a convenient, efficient way of reaching the best musical results.

The use of the arms in playing this music is a matter of utmost importance, but unfortunately it can't be indicated in the music in any practical, comprehensible way.

The use of the damper pedal for this music is also a matter of greatest importance, though Rachmaninoff seldom indicated pedaling. He wrote it for unusual passages, and completely for only one piece, leaving the large part of his piano music without pedal indications. Good pedaling has to be coordinated with fingering, and is dependent on the resonance of the piano, the reflected sound from the room, the tempos, the dynamic levels and balances involved, and the skill of the performer. Though the modern way of indicating pedaling is an improvement over the older pedal indications (Ped. *), it is not completely satisfactory, since some of the most beautiful and subtle pedaling results from depressing the pedal to different depths. Particularly important is the technique of depressing the pedal barely enough to lift the dampers off the strings so that changes can be accomplished with maximum speed. The kind of half pedaling which briefly seats the dampers so lightly on the strings that the upper strings are damped while the lower strings continue to sound is also of great value. These refined pedal effects are impossible to notate in the music. They must be arrived at by experiment and careful listening during practice. The pedaling given here should serve the student during the learning process and should be a point of departure for later, more subtle use of the damper pedal.

# GENERAL SUGGESTIONS

Trills in Rachmaninoff's music start on the given note, not on the upper auxiliary as in the music of the 18th century. Rolled chords are frequent and should be done with minimum disruption of the rhythmic pulse. With few exceptions broadening the tempo as the music moves toward the rolled chord is desirable, so that the lowest notes of the chord start slightly early, and the top note arrives on the delayed beat. If the rolled chord starts in the bass the pedal should go down on the lowest note before the finger leaves the key, so that the lowest note—the harmonic bass for the rest of the chord—continues to sound. People with large hands can often play large rolled chords by relaxing the wrist and each finger after it has played its key, while swinging the elbow to the right, usually with a high wrist. People with average or small hands must experiment to find the best way for them to roll these widely spaced chords. Some will find it easiest to start a right hand four-or five-note rolled chord spanning a tenth with the second finger, the thumb and other fingers following upward in the obvious order. This is particularly true if the tempo is not fast. Other people will find it easier to start such a chord with the thumb and put the third or fourth finger over the fifth at the top of the chord. This is particularly useful if the top note is a black key which follows a white. However they are played, these chords should sound graceful rather than strained, should fit the dynamic context, and should be evenly balanced dynamically with all the sounds equidistant in time. These and other works can best be studied, memorized, and performed if the form of the music is clear in the player's mind. In other words, if the student sees how the composer has put the piece together he or she is better able to practice it intelligently (using sections and subsections for practice segments), memorize it efficiently, and concentrate on it during the performance. The interpretation of the music will be more convincing if matters of form are understood, since interpreting music is concerned with clarifying for the listener similarities and differences in the music. Rachmaninoff's early works usually have clear-cut sections and subsections, but in the later works these points of arrival and departure are often disguised by subtle craftsmanship which makes the piece flow connectedly from beginning to end but which obscures the articulations for the learner. The brief analyses which follow, together with practice suggestions, should help persons unfamiliar with these pieces to begin their study effectively.

# THE PIECES

## *ELÉGIE IN E-FLAT MINOR, No. 1* — *Page 8*

This dark-hued piece, by its key and placement on the keyboard takes advantage of rich piano resonance and exploits fully the expressive qualities of the instrument. The melody which begins the piece and returns in embellished versions is characterized by syncopations that suggest the imbalance of great sorrow. The gloom of E-flat minor is lightened by the middle section in the relative major whose fragmentary melodies change from cello to flute registers before reaching a full-bodied Lisztian climax. The meditative transitional passage, which leads back to the opening melody enriched by doublings, ends with a coda which might indicate a swift descent into despair and the upward sweep of an anguished cry.

The facilitations in this edition indicate a way of avoiding some awkward hand crossings, though of course, left hand accompaniment notes played by the right should be in the same dynamic level as the rest of the harmonic background. Measure 104, misinterpreted in several other editions (it has been divided into two measures or printed as a double length measure), should in its quickened rhythmic patterns occur in the same amount of time as the previous measure. Practicing the left hand measures 103 and 104 consecutively while counting two to a bar helps solve the problem. Before starting the piece the sostenuto pedal may be set silently on the low E-flat and held for the first six measures. Rachmaninoff sometimes played the first measure *forte* and then made a diminuendo to *pianissimo* in the second measure.

## *PRELUDE IN C-SHARP MINOR, No. 2* — *Page 14*

Rachmaninoff denied that he had any descriptive idea in mind when he wrote this prelude, though it is not surprising that people have thought so, because the music immediately establishes a mood of great seriousness. Sustaining the whole and half notes on the first page is a problem best solved by the use of the sostenuto pedal, but since many pianos do not have this expensive device, the first page is printed here with an alternate version in which the left hand little finger can quickly take one of the low notes played by the right hand, to hold it while half pedaling retains part of the sound of the lowest bass notes.

The tempo set by the three opening notes should be held steady up to measure 14. The middle section is faster as indicated, and the up-stemmed melody notes should stand out against the bass line while the second and third notes of the triplet are softer. The right hand part can be practiced by blocking the chords—playing all the notes on one beat at the same time (except for those places as in measure 17 where there is an up-stemmed eighth note, which can be played after the chord)—as far as the middle of measure 35. At the end of measures 27, 28, 30, and 31 it is necessary to broaden the beats so that the long jump for the left hand won't give the rhythm a disturbing wrench. The cadenza of interlocked chords which begins in measure 35 can also be practiced by playing simultaneously all the notes on one beat. By this means the sound of the chords and the feel of the keyboard positions are clearly established in the student's mind before the accents alternating between the hands introduce a further complication. Measures 43 and 44 establish by augmentation the opening motif and should re-establish the original tempo.

From measure 45, when four staves are used simultaneously, maximum sonority can be achieved only by using maximum weight of the arm. Again at the end of measure 50 and measure 52 the tempo must be broadened so that the continuity of the pulse is bent but not broken, as both hands move from the low to the high chords written on the first beat. The coda, which begins at measure 55, may be done with a diminuendo; since all the chords have C-sharps in addition to the low C-sharps (the pedal-point in the bass), the new elements in each chord may be stressed lightly.

### *MÉLODIE IN E MAJOR,* No. 3
*(original version)* *Page 20*

A left hand melody that might be played by a cello starts this piece with an eight-measure phrase which soars to its high note and then drifts downward to a cadence. It is followed by a varied version in octaves with fuller accompaniment though the harmony moves to A-flat to end the phrase. The middle section begins at measure 18 with two-measure phrases in A-flat and B, but at measure 26 the pace of harmonic change quickens and phrases implying E-flat, F-sharp, B-flat, F, E, and C approach a sudden cessation of motion which introduces the third section. Beginning at measure 41, the original melody is restated in an opulent new version after which the middle section is recalled in the tonic key. A quiet coda, starting at measure 51, moves to a delicate, exquisitely spaced final chord.

This edition, by using some unconventional divisions of notes between the hands and careful pedaling, makes the sustaining of some of the long bass notes possible and makes some of the playing less difficult.

At measures 44 through 47 there are melody notes in octaves that can only be held to their full notated value without blurring by the use of a sostenuto pedal. These notes are marked with the press and release signs Ⓢ and *. If a sostenuto pedal isn't available careful shading can make these notes go on in the imagination to link with the following notes in the melodic line.

### *POLICHINELLE IN F-SHARP MINOR, No. 4* *Page 26*

The name of this piece means *Punch*, a character in the Punch and Judy puppet shows popular years ago in many parts of Europe. Traditionally, Punch was an ugly puppet with a hump back and hook nose and chin, who boasted a great deal and beat his nagging wife. As the music begins one can imagine him jumping onto the stage, moving with a shuffle to disappear on the opposite side, and then repeating the action from the opposite direction. After the introduction (as the play begins) it is easy to hear in the music his alternate loud boasting, sly threats, and terrible rages.

The form of this piece is clearly ternary. Bringing out the melody in the middle section, which begins at measure 59, is not difficult since the melody is doubled in the lower octave, but the student should be concerned in this section with shaping each of the four-measure phrases to emphasize the longer notes. The return of the first section, abbreviated but amplified with thicker chords, is the most difficult part of the piece, particularly for those with small hands.

### *SÉRÉNADE IN B-FLAT MINOR,* No. 5
*(Original version)* *Page 36*

This piece summons up an atmosphere of Spain and a love song being sung with guitar accompaniment. It starts with a feeling of delightful uncertainty because a root position tonic chord does not occur until measure 59. The introduction has the quality of an improvisation before the song proper begins at measure 31. An interlude with seductive chromatic harmony begins at measure 62. At measure 74 the song is continued with interruptions from the interlude, and the piece moves forward with song and interlude alternating. The song has been in the range of a tenor voice until measure 110, but there it goes into a higher octave. Does this mean that the lady, after a hesitant beginning, replies with her version of the song? What is the meaning of the coda, with 17 measures of delicate interlude and a very loud final measure? A simple surprise, or a triumph?

# Morceaux de Fantaisie

## (Fantasy Pieces)

to Anton Arensky

# ELÉGIE in E-flat minor

Op. 3, No. 1
(1892)

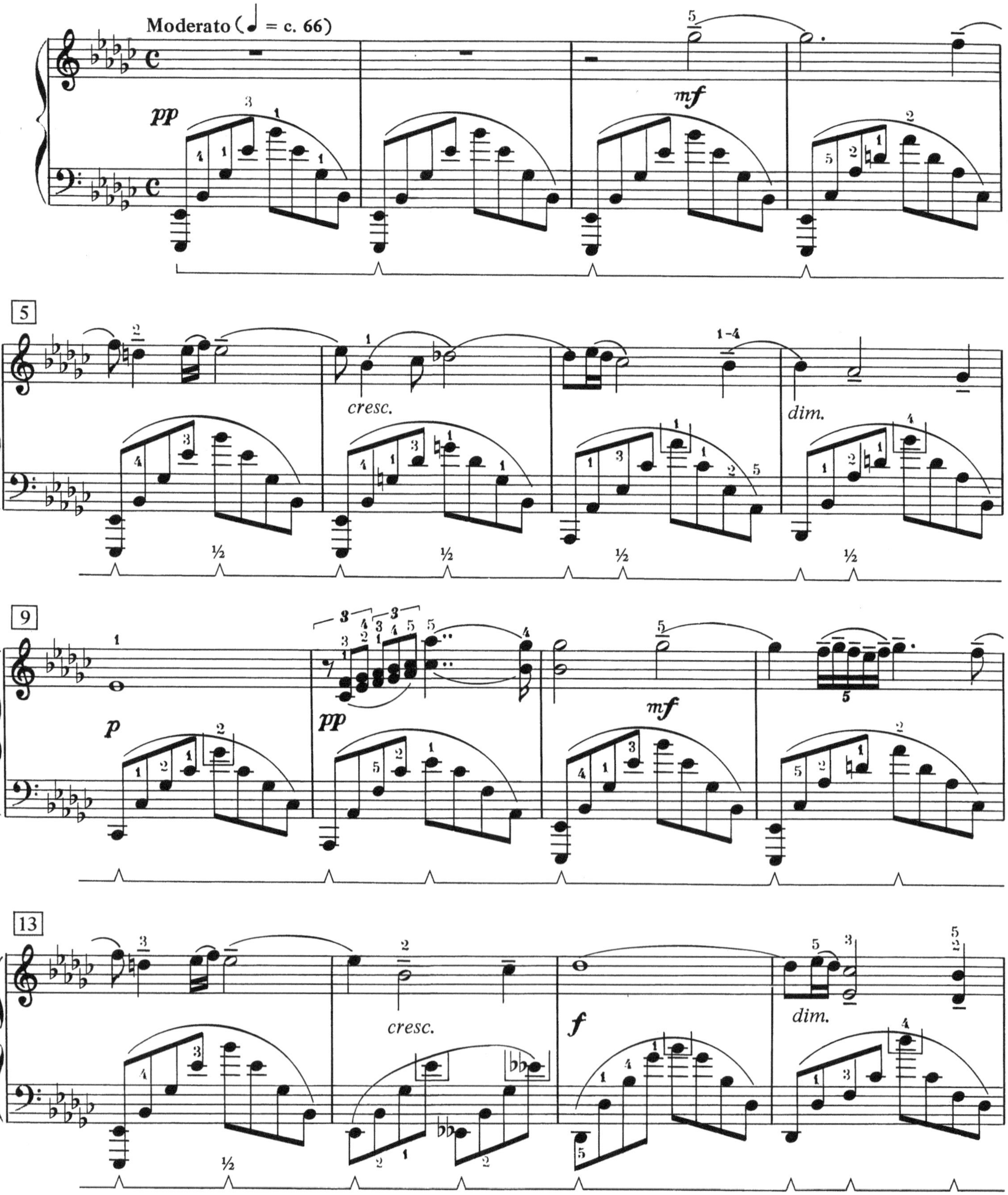

17
p
pp
21
con affetto
cresc.
25
ff
29
dim.

33
37
rit.
41
Più vivo ( = c. 54 )
45

49
rit.
53
a tempo
mf
pp
57
mf
pp
L.H.
R.H.
61
cresc.
pp
65
cresc.

69
8va
fff
appassionato
73
8va
77
ff
81
(Lento)
R.H.
L.H.
p
(a piacere)
p
84
Tempo I
pp

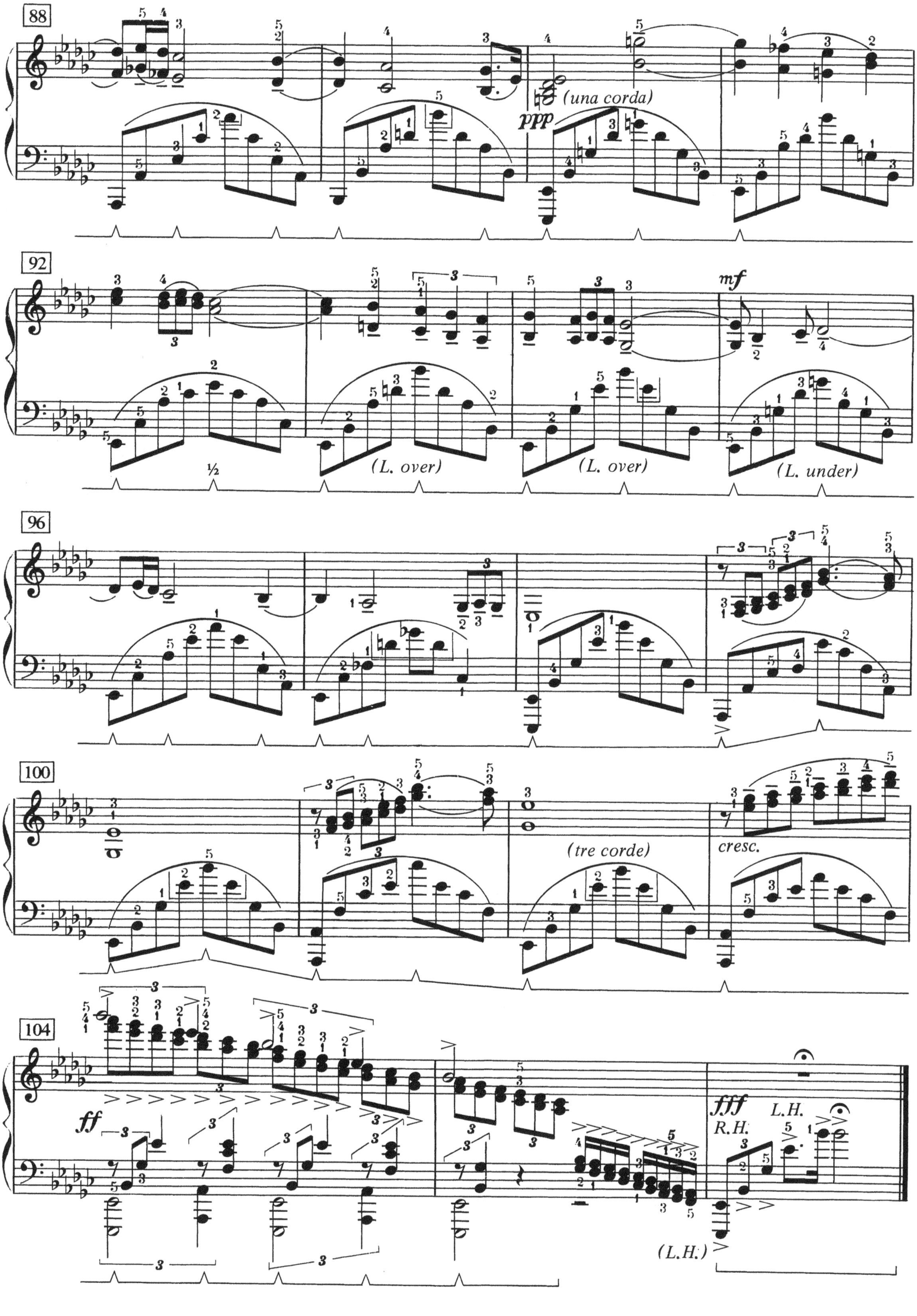
88
(una corda)
ppp
92
½
(L. over)
(L. over)
mf
(L. under)
96
100
(tre corde)
cresc.
104
ff
fff
R.H.
L.H.
(L.H.)

# PRELUDE in C-sharp minor

(the first 13 measures for pianos without a sostenuto pedal) (Half-pedal carefully)

Op. 3, No. 2
(1892)

# PRELUDE in C-sharp minor

For pianos with a sostenuto pedal

Ⓢ = depress sostenuto after keys are down

* = release sostenuto

**Op. 3, No. 2**
**(1892)**

① Although it has often been printed, recorded, and misread as D natural, the D-sharp in the left hand, here and in measure 48, is correct.

14
Agitato (♩ = c. 104-156)
mf
cresc.
17
dim.
mf
20
cresc.
23
dim.
cresc.

26
ff
half ped.
Ped. sim.
29
dim.
32
cresc.
35
accel.
fff

38
41
ff
(rit.)
sfff
Tempo I
45
fff pesante
sffff

48
sffff
sffff
51
dim.
dim.
54
dim.
mf
ppp
dim.
mf
ppp

# MÉLODIE in E major

*(original version)*

**Op. 3, No. 3**
**(1892)**

**Adagio sostenuto** (♩ = c. 58)

12
cresc.
ff
dim.
15
dim.
17
p
mf
pp
19

21
cresc.
23
25
R.H.
27
R.H.
R.H.

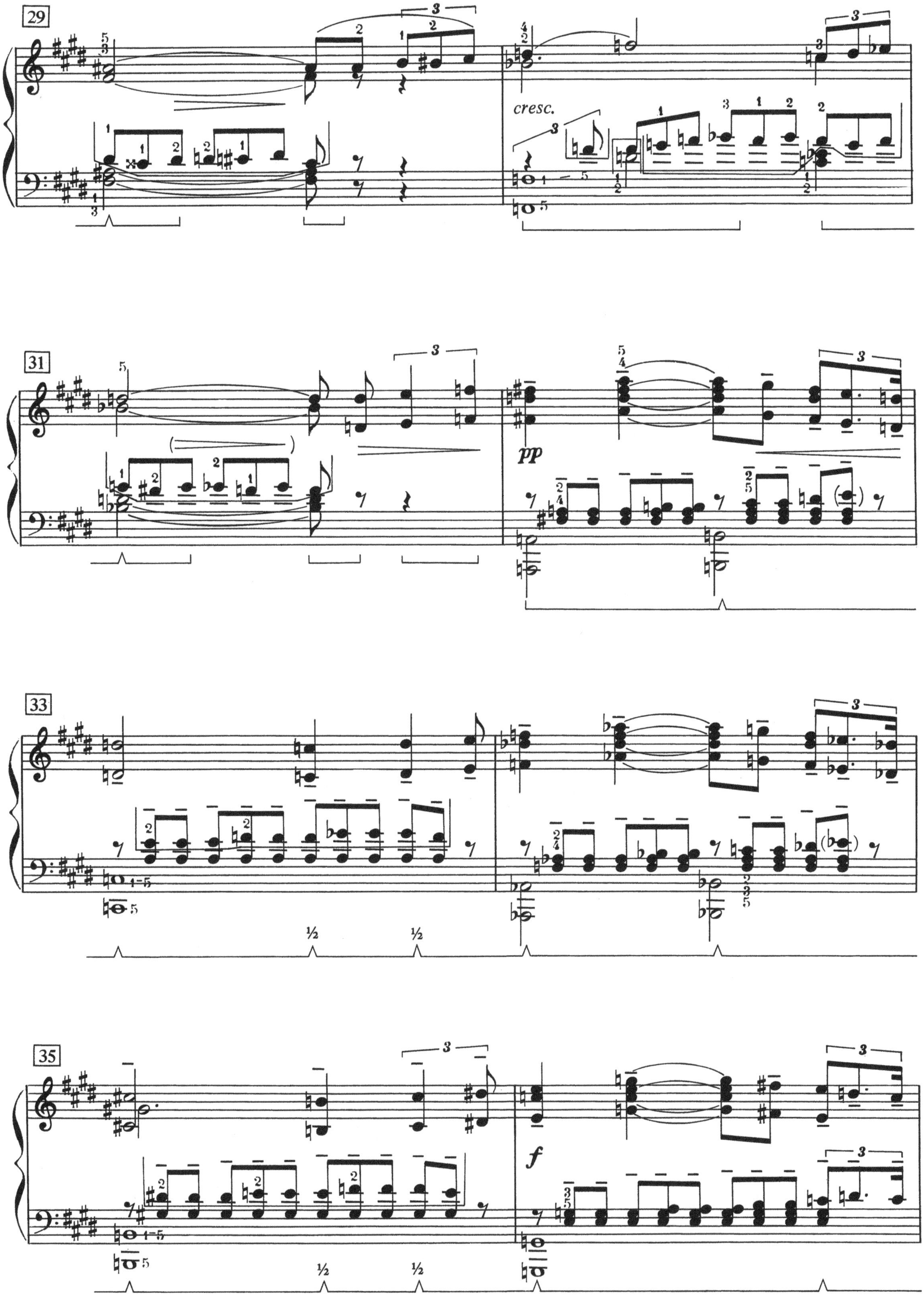
29
cresc.
31
pp
33
35
f

37
mf
40
p
pp
ppp
p
43
cresc.
ppp
46

48
pp
p
50
52
54
dim.
57
rit.
ppp (a piacere)

# POLICHINELLE in F-sharp minor

Op. 3, No. 4
(1892)

Allegro vivace (♩ = c.152)

* Usually played

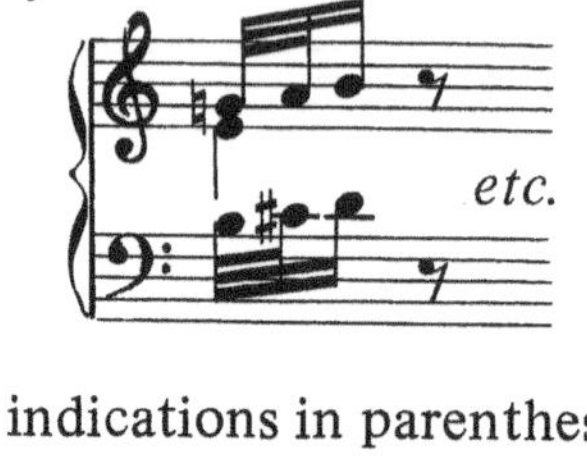


** The *forte* indications in parentheses in measures 3, 7, 94, and 98 do not appear in the Russian editions.

17
ff
21
p
ff
25
p
ff
28
8va
sfff

31
8va
8va
sfff
34
36
p
ff
40
p

44
ff
p
47
8va
ff
50
8va
sfff
sfff
53
8va

55
59
Agitato
f
62
65
dim.
p

68
p
pp
71
f
74
77
dim.
p

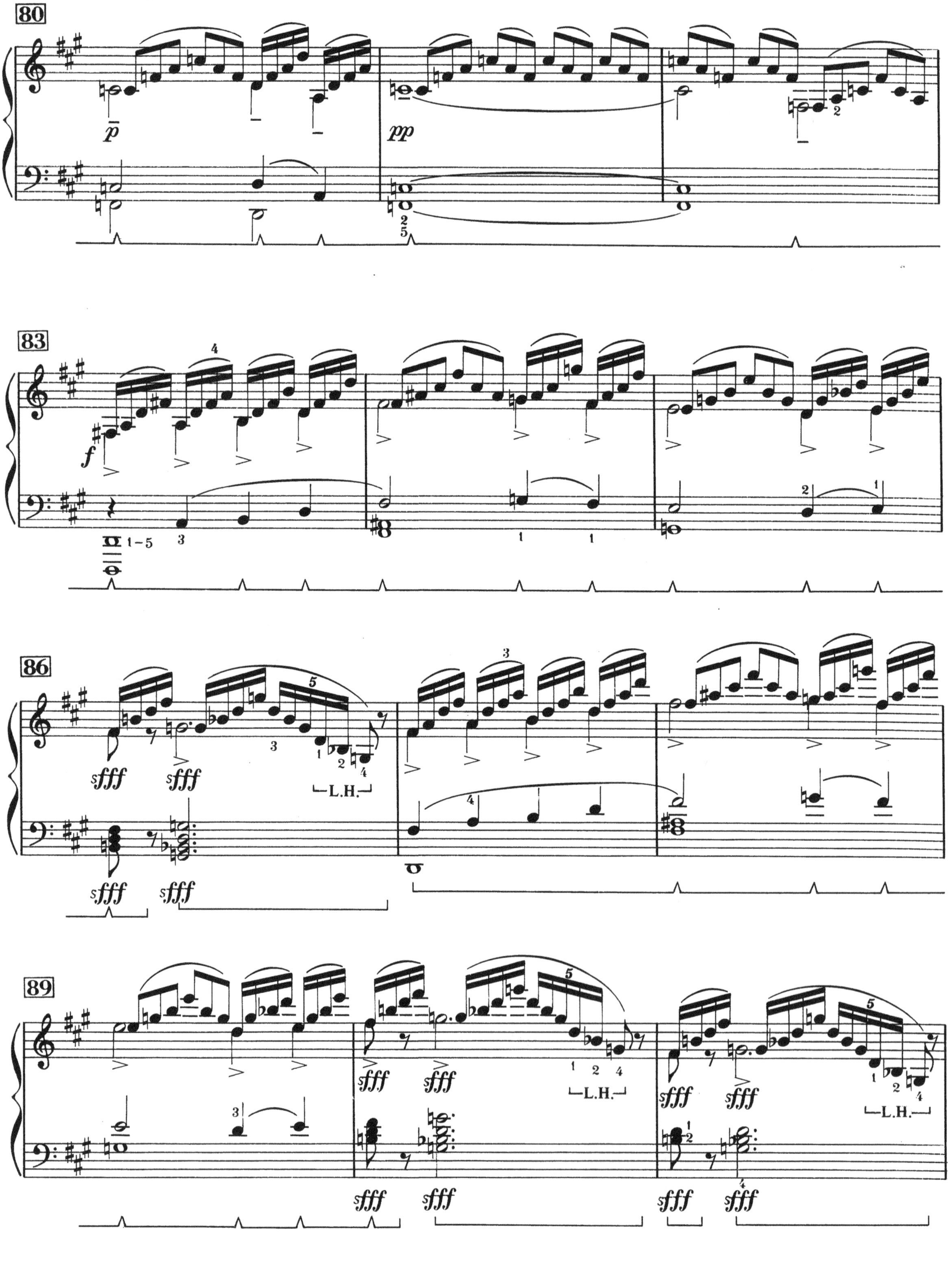
80
p
pp
83
f
86
sfff
L.H.
89
sfff
L.H.
L.H.

92
sfff
sfff
ppp
(f)
sfff
sfff
sfff
sfff
sfff
sfff
96
p
(f)
101
ff
105
f

109
fff
112
f
115
8va
fff
f
118
ff
8va

121
8va
sfff
123
8va
sfff
125
8va
127
8va
fff
8va

# SÉRÉNADE in B-flat minor

*(original version)*

Op. 3, No. 5
(1892)

* In a recording Rachmaninoff played several passages of this piece with embellishments.

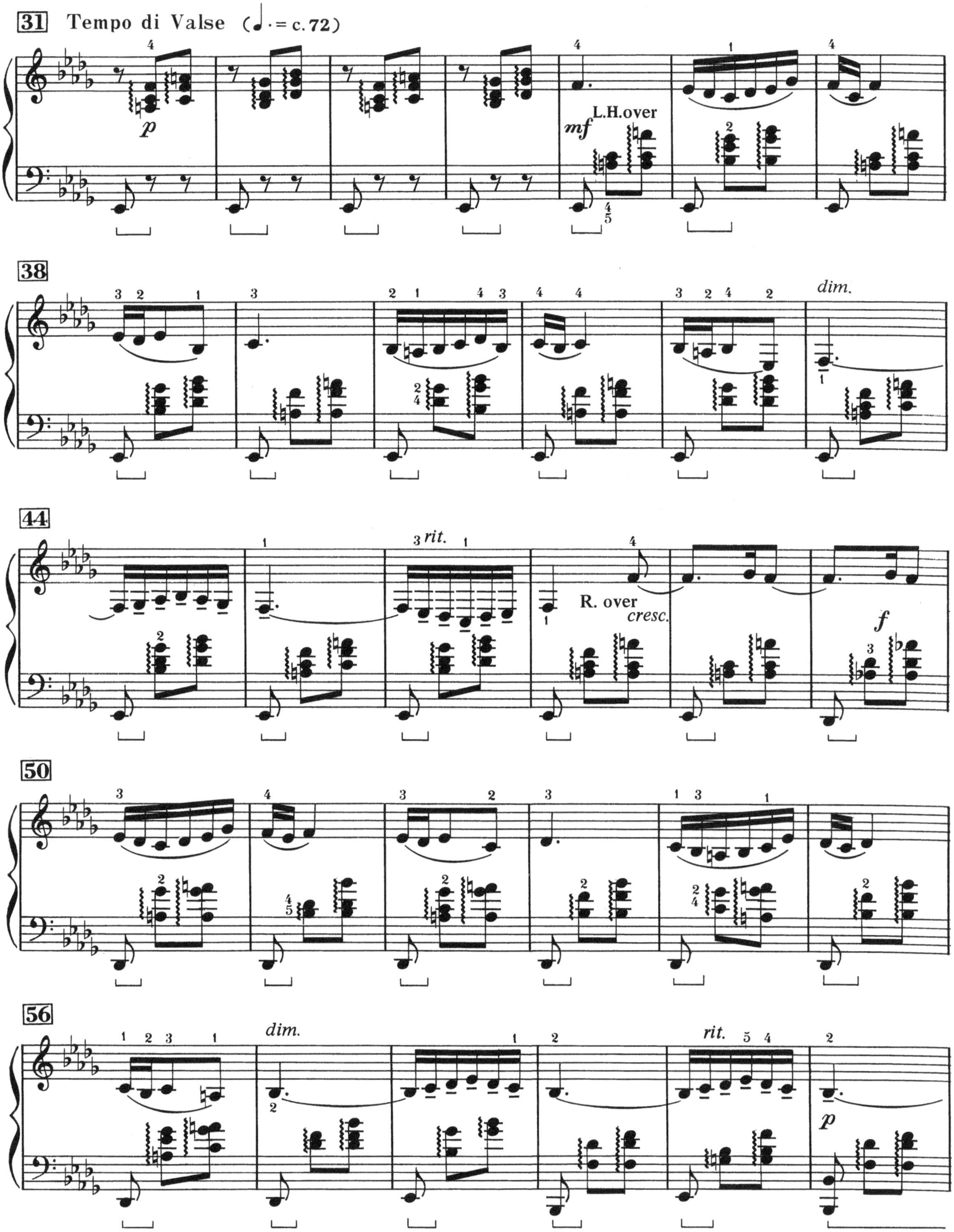
31
Tempo di Valse (♩. = c. 72)
p
mf
L.H.over
38
dim.
44
rit.
R. over
cresc.
f
50
56
dim.
rit.
p

* The Siloti edition omits the downstemmed F's for the right hand in measures 88 and 89, tied from measure 87.

90
pp
ppp
98
pppp
cresc.
105
dim.
mf
p
112
118
dim.
rit.

*In measure 127 Siloti omits the top G-flat of the L.H. chord on the second beat.
**In measure 142 the B-flats for the L.H. on the second and third beats are also omitted by Siloti.